THIS BOOK BELONGS TO:

BY THE BOCKBORN

The Letter A

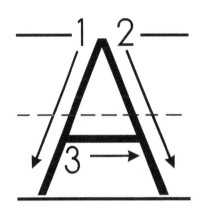 

A is for

ANT-MAN

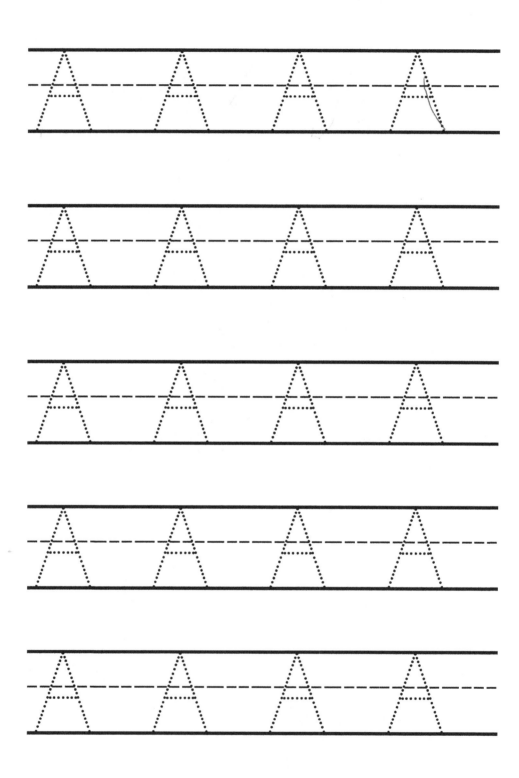

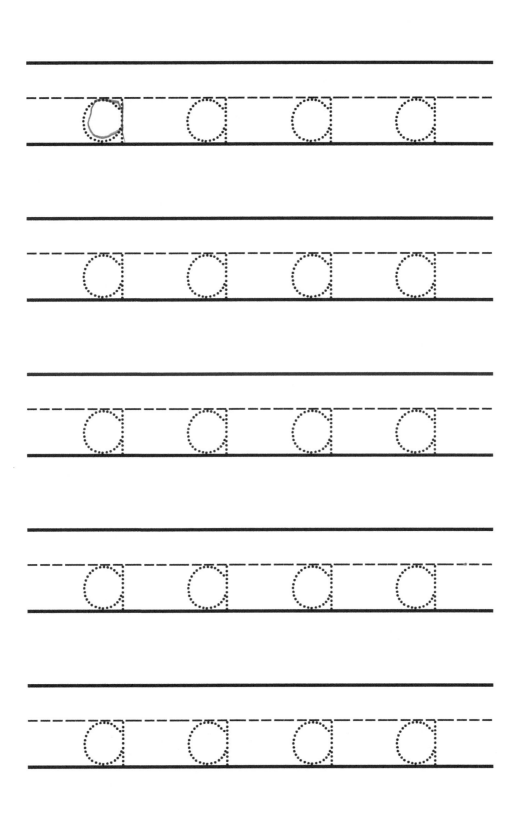

The Letter B

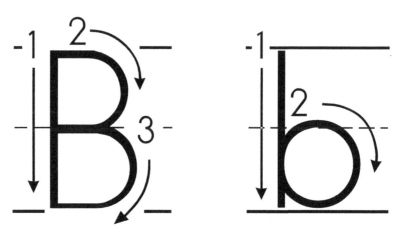

 **B** is for

BATMAN

BBBB

BBBB

BBBB

BBBB

BBBB

The Letter C

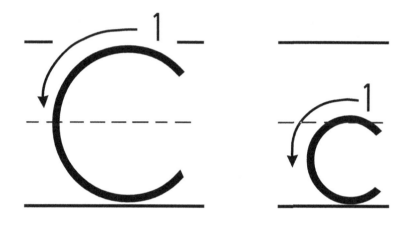

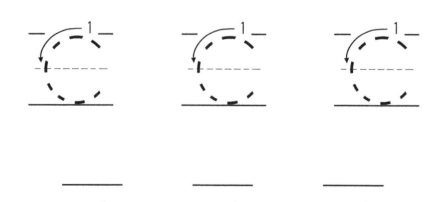

 is for

CAPTAIN AMERICA

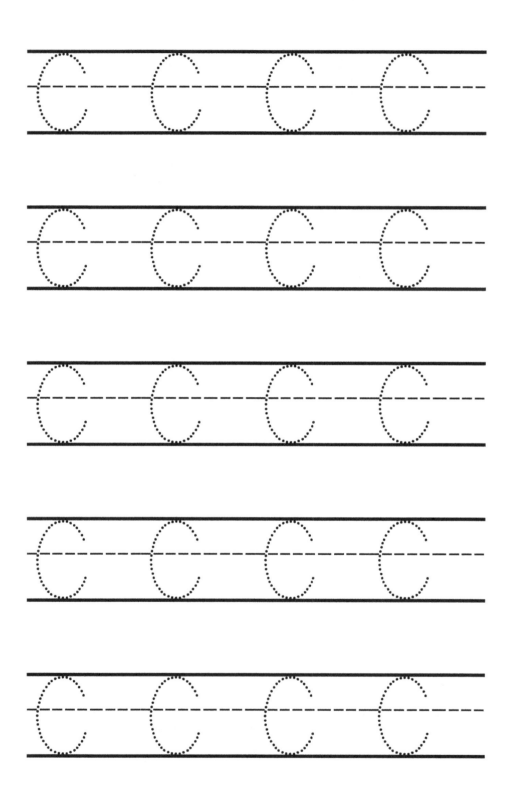

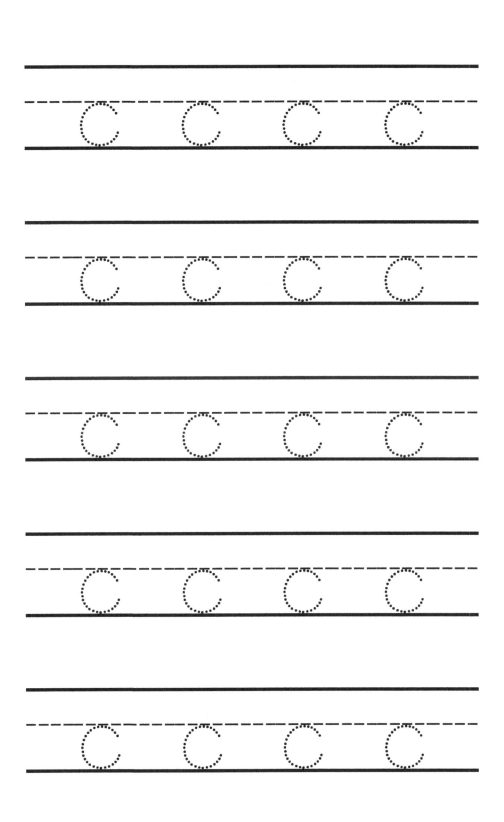

The Letter D

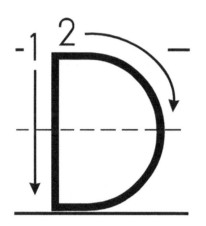 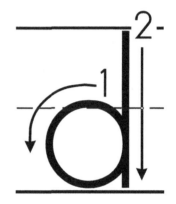

D is for

DAREDEVIL

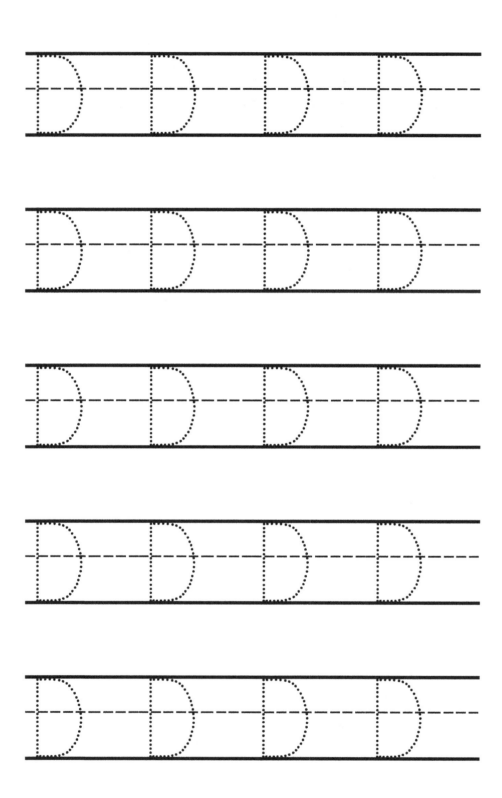

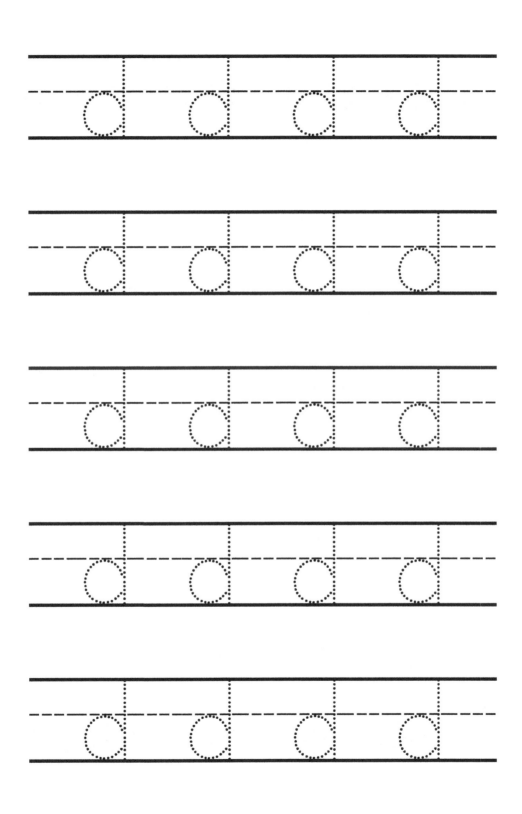

The Letter E

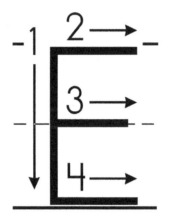 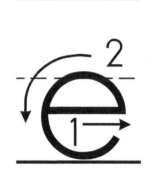

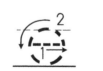 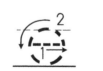 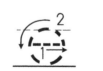

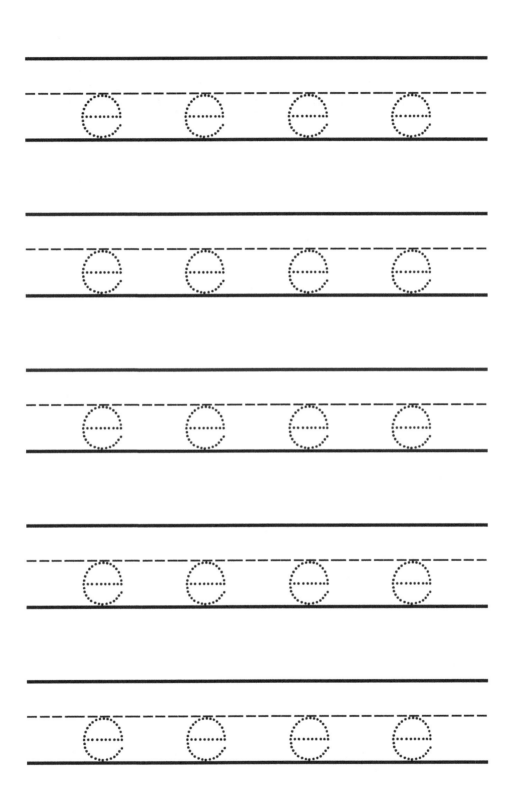

The Letter F

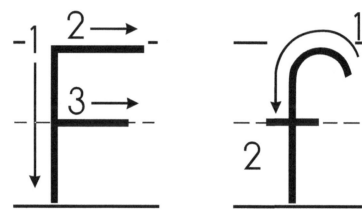

F is for

FLASH

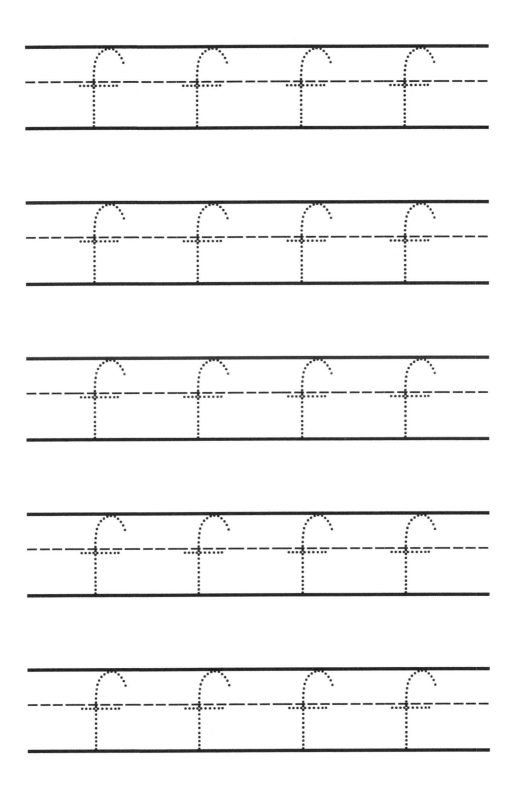

The Letter G

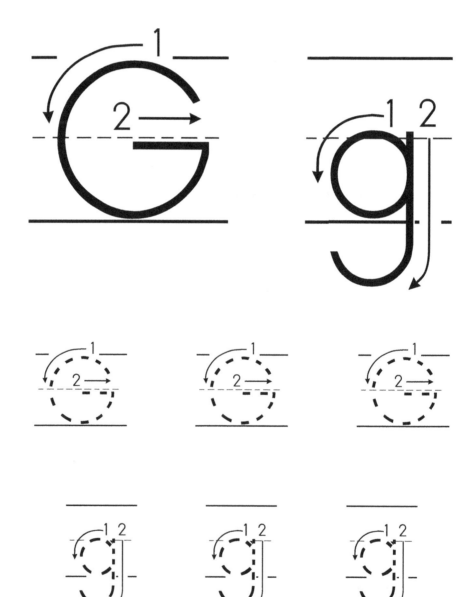

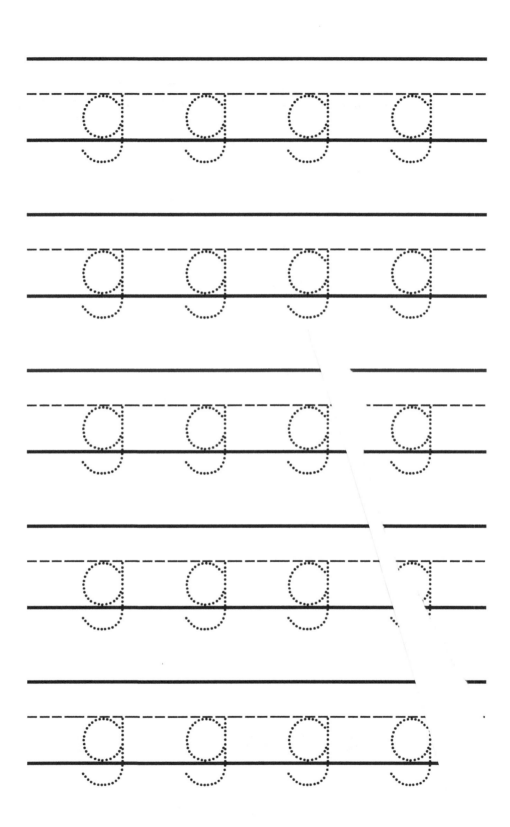

The Letter H

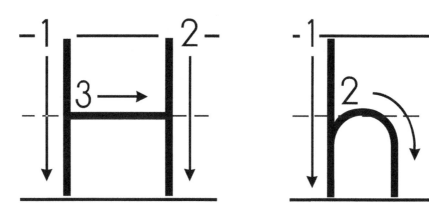
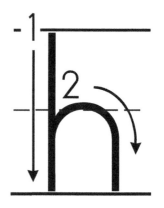

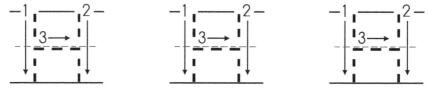

H is for

HULK

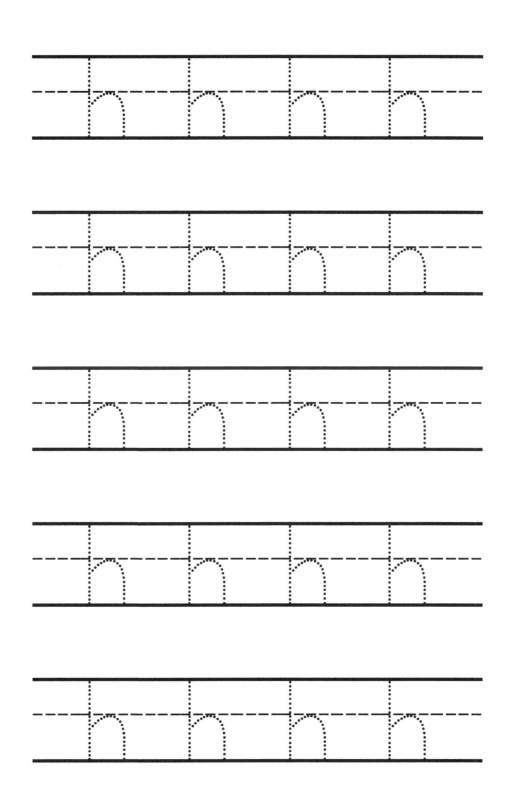

The Letter I

I is for

IRON MAN

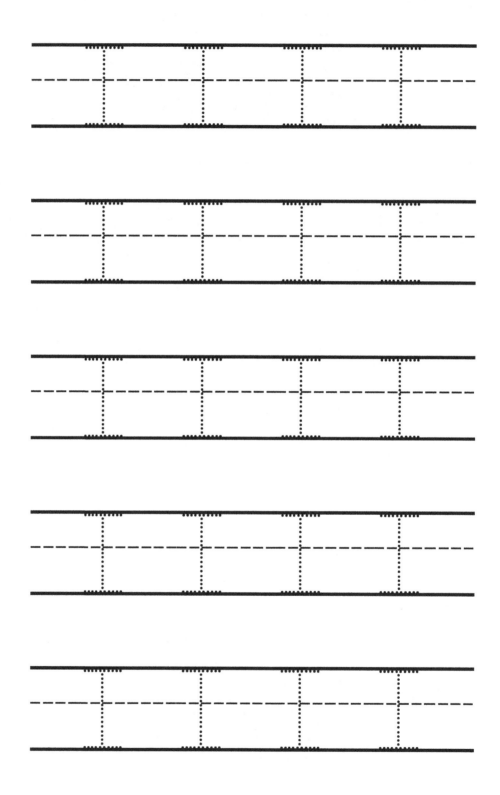

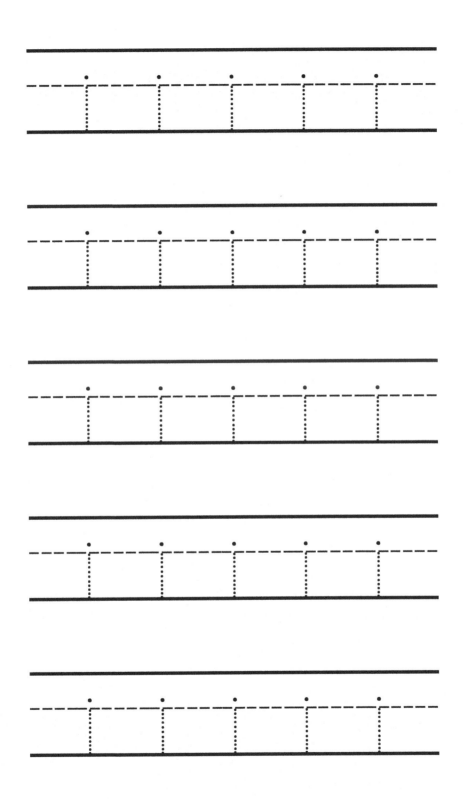

The Letter J

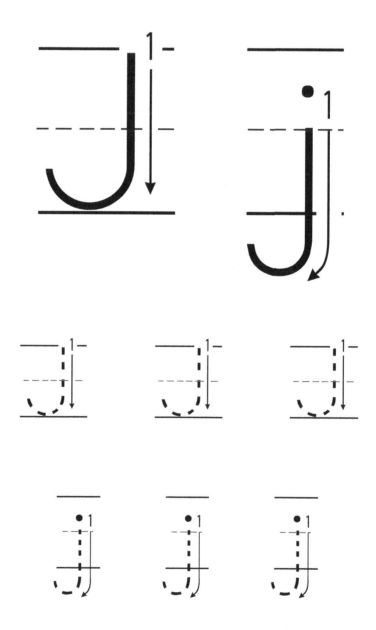

J is for

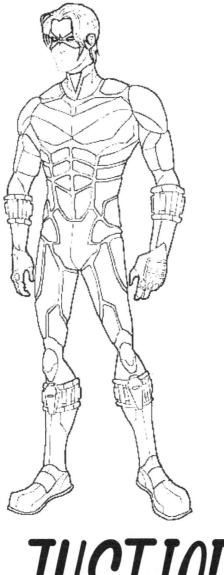

JUSTICE

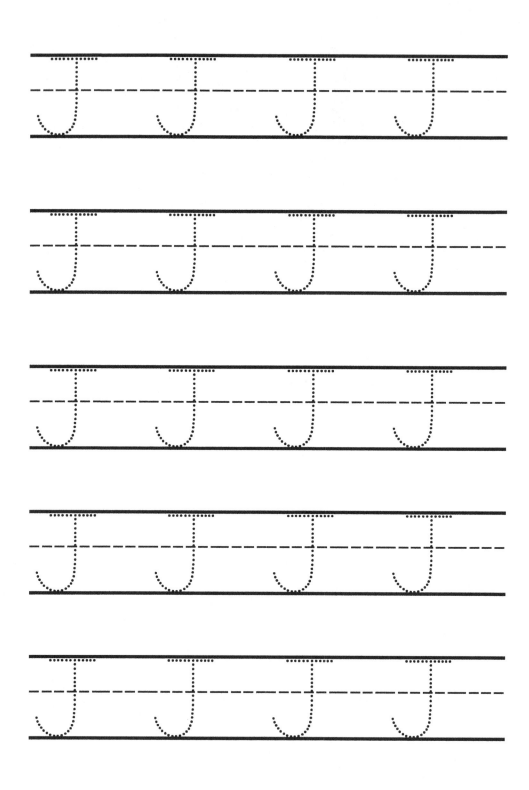

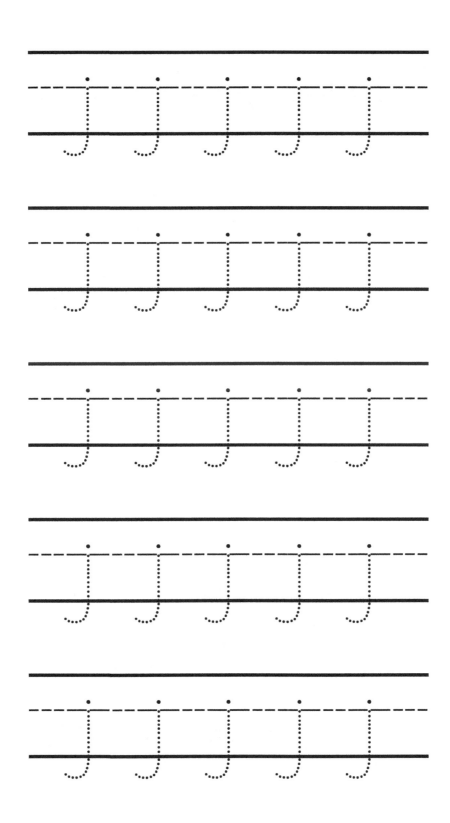

The Letter K

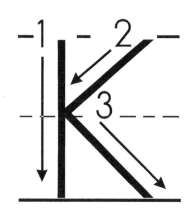 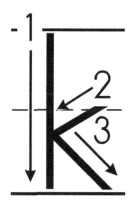

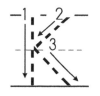 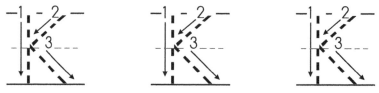

K is for

KRYPTO

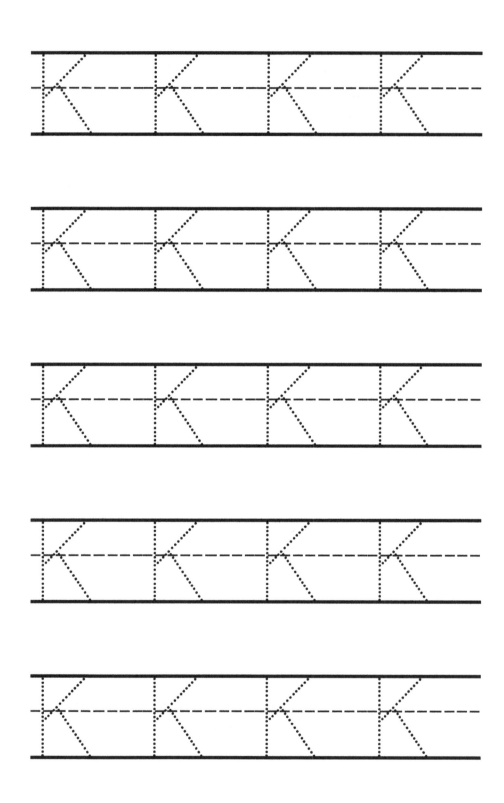

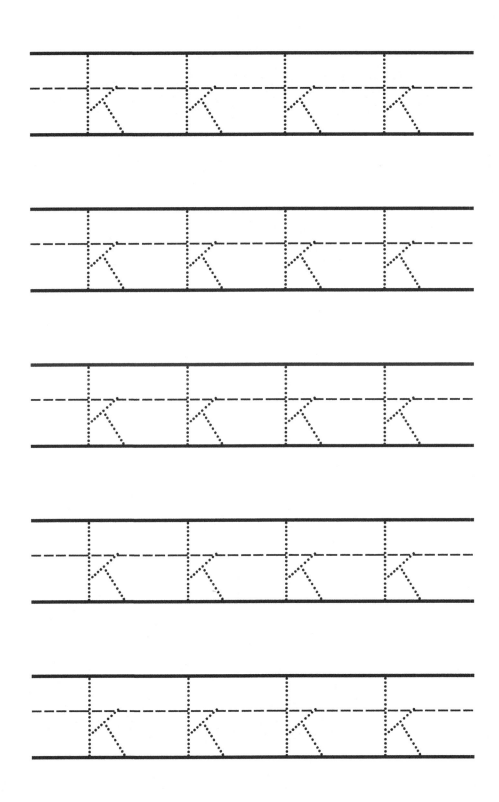

The Letter L

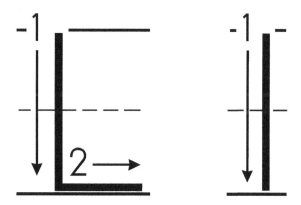

 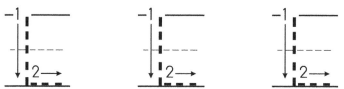

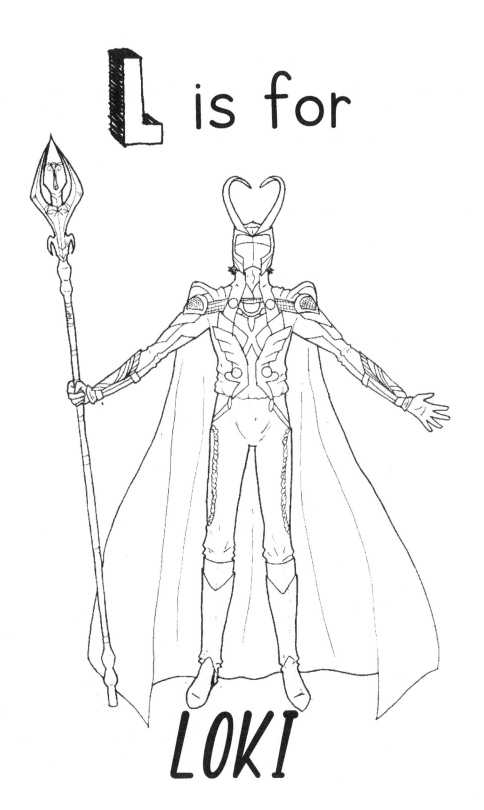

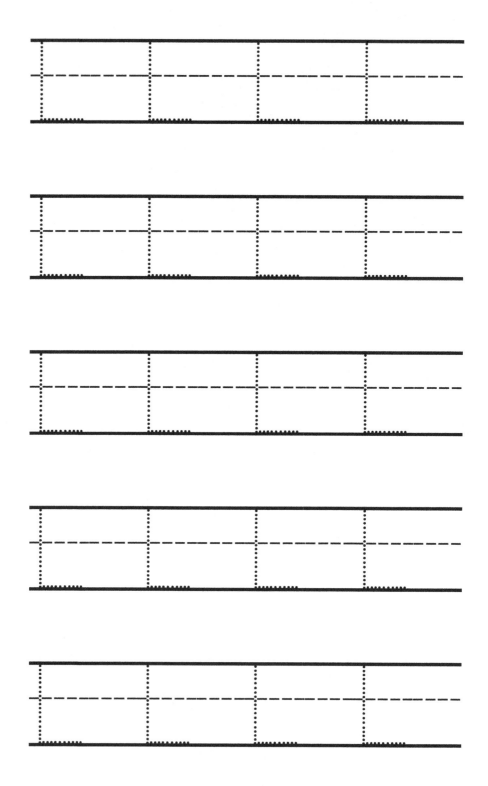

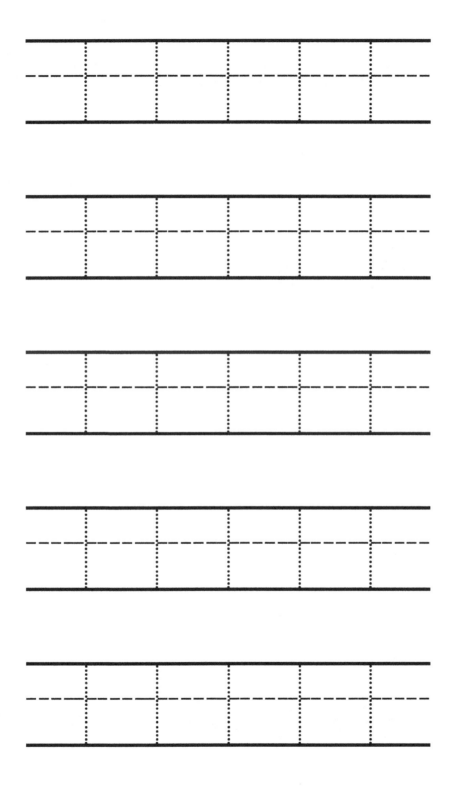

The Letter M

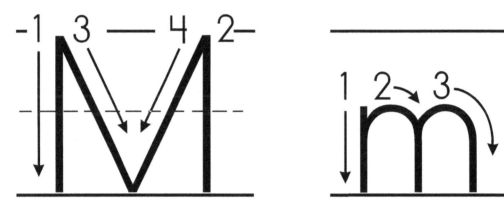

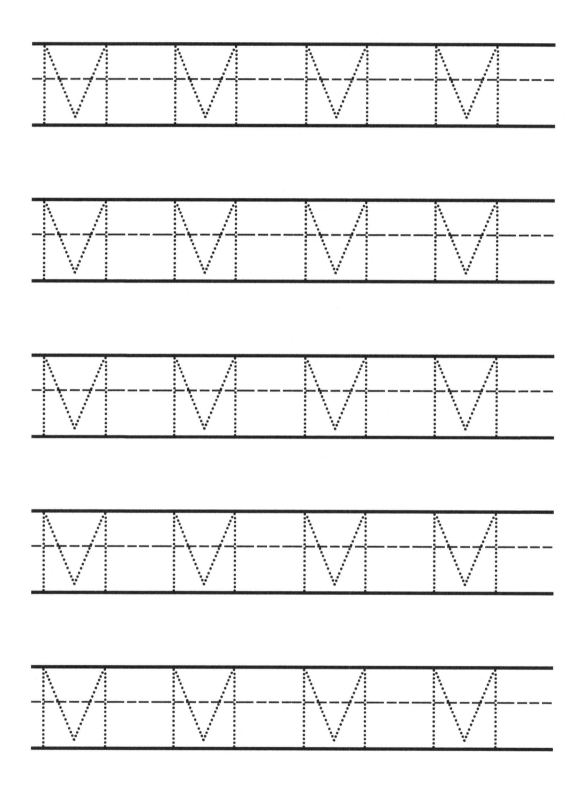

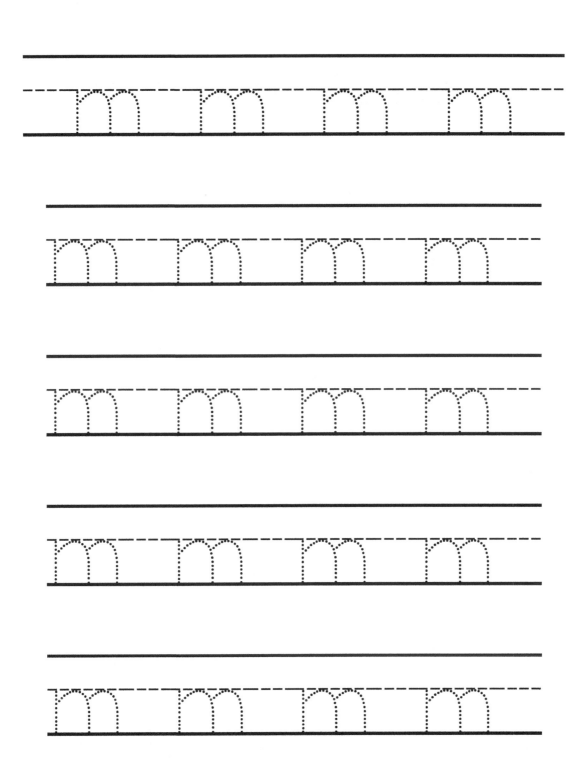

The Letter N

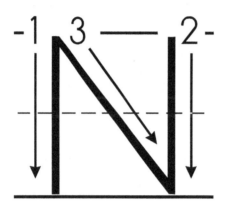 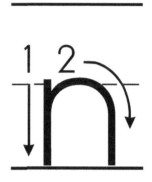

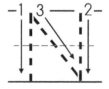 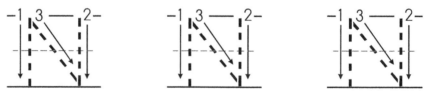

N is for

NIGHTCRAWLER

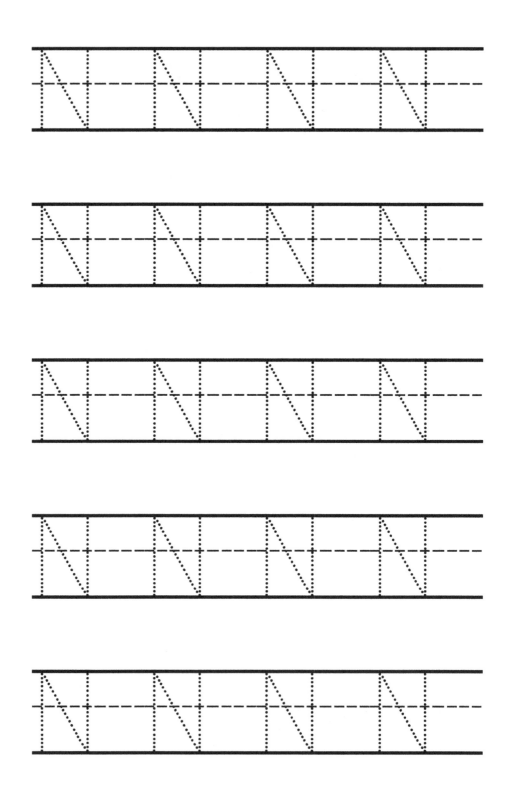

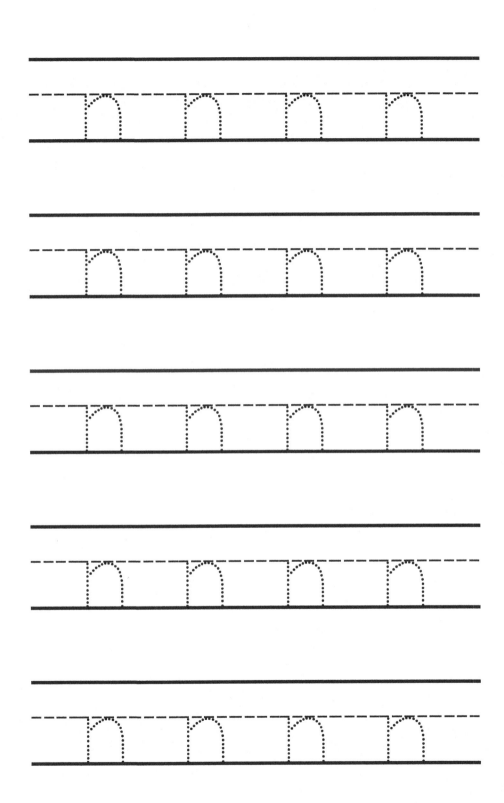

The Letter O

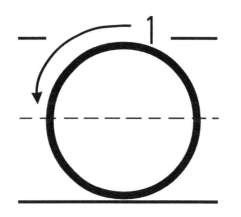
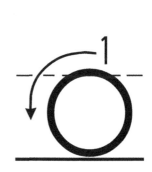
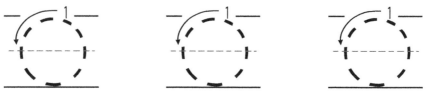

O is for

ODIN

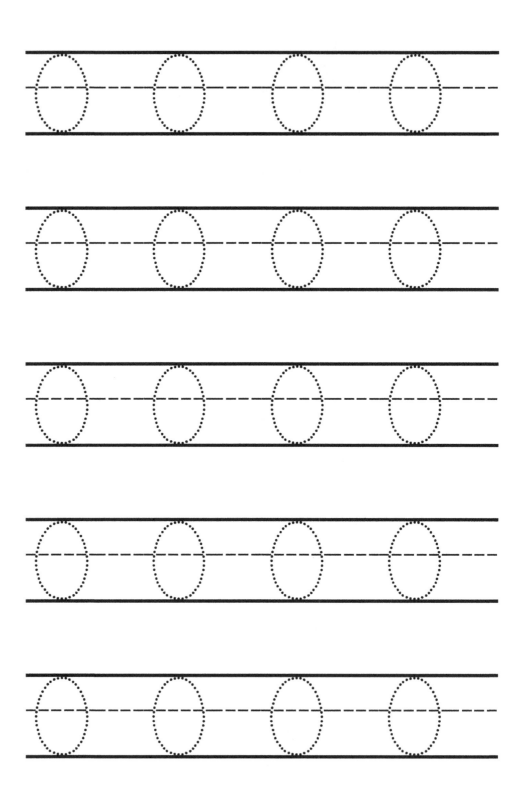

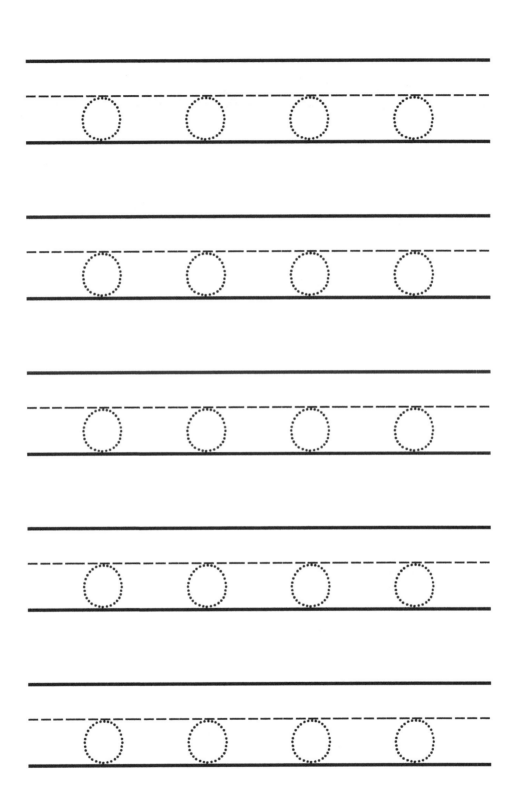

The Letter P

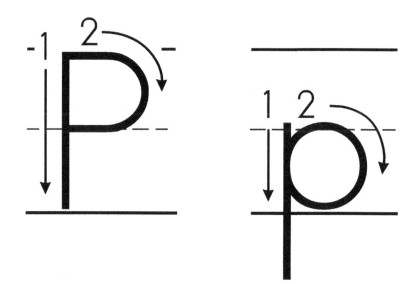

 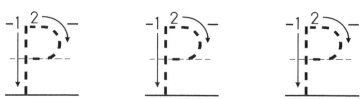

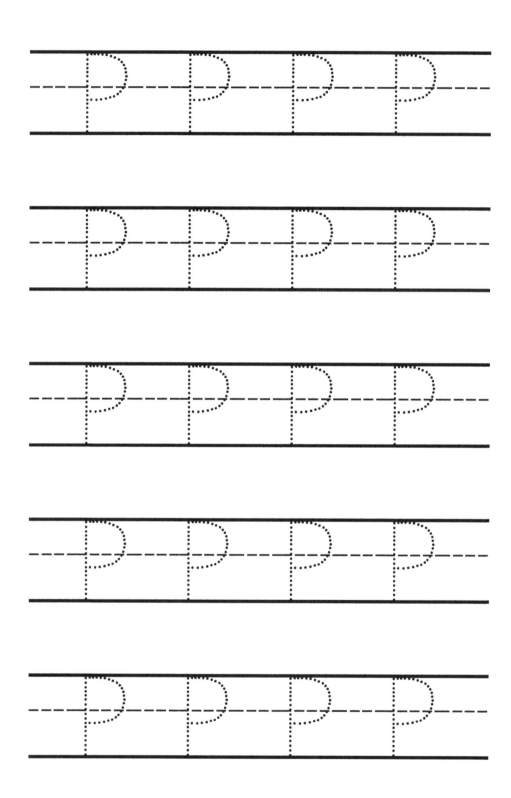

The Letter Q

Q is for

QUICKSILVER

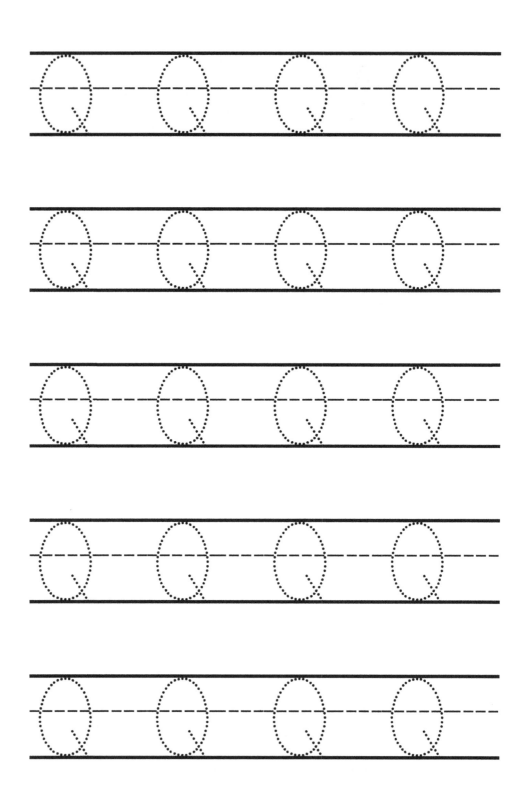

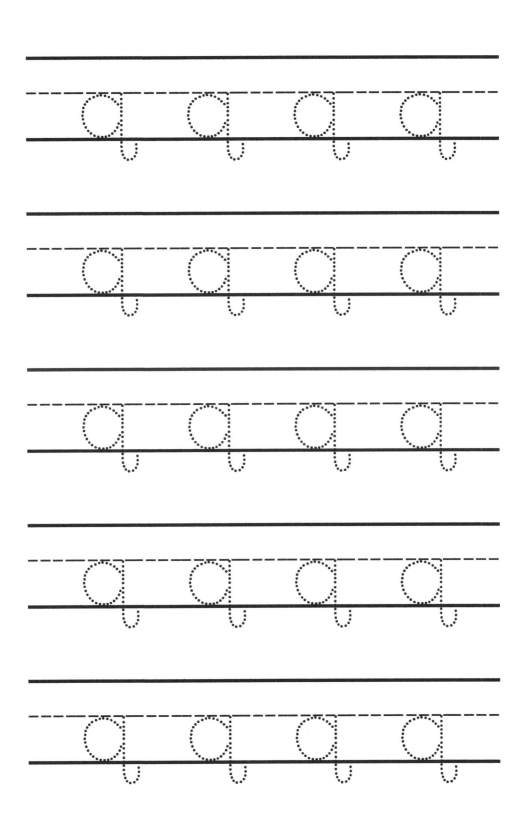

The Letter R

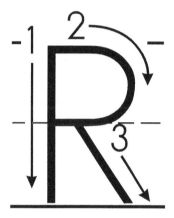

R is for

ROBIN

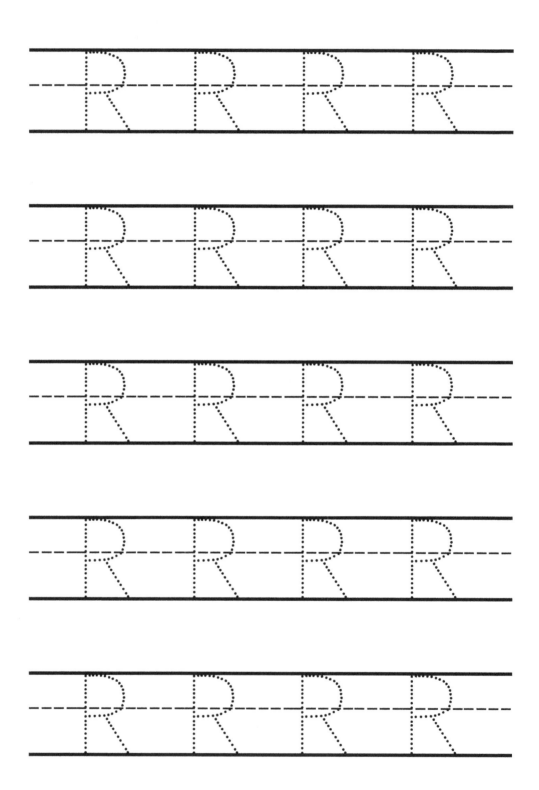

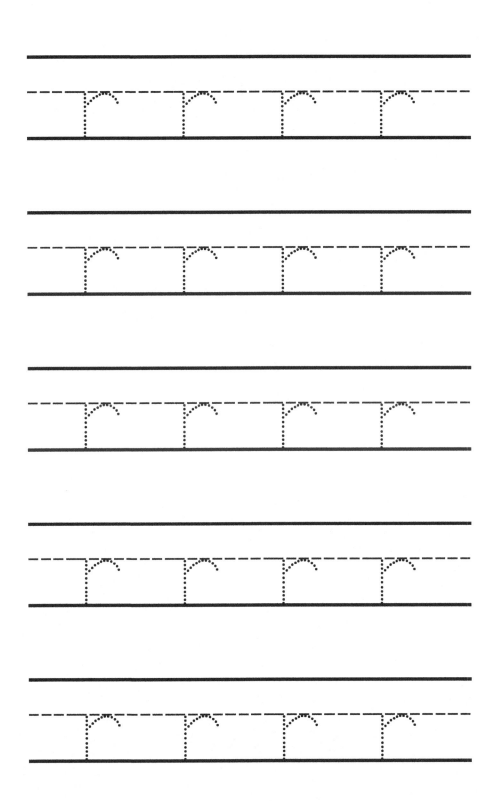

The Letter S

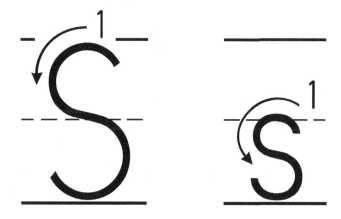

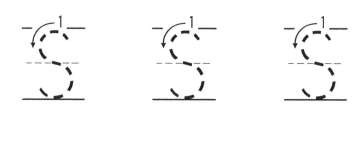

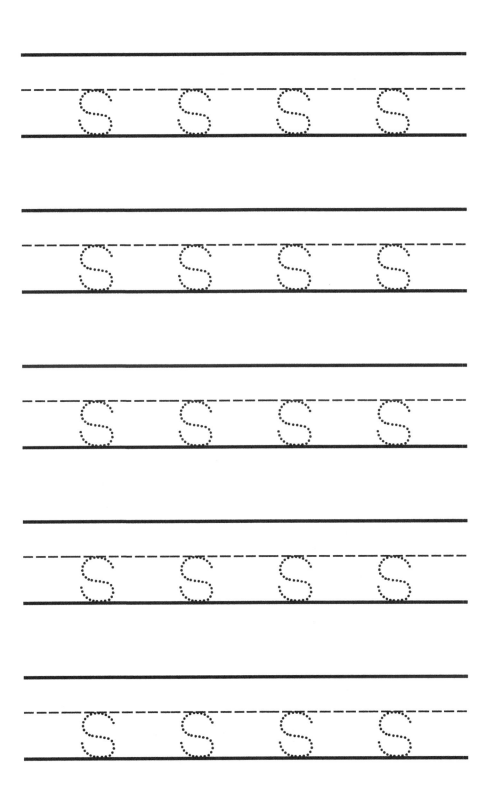

The Letter T

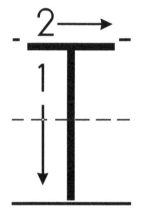 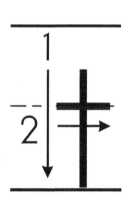

T is for

THOR

The Letter U

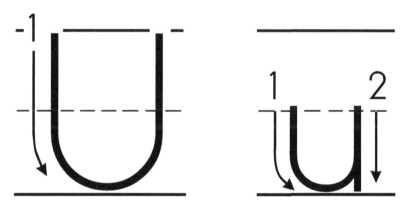

U is for

ULTRON

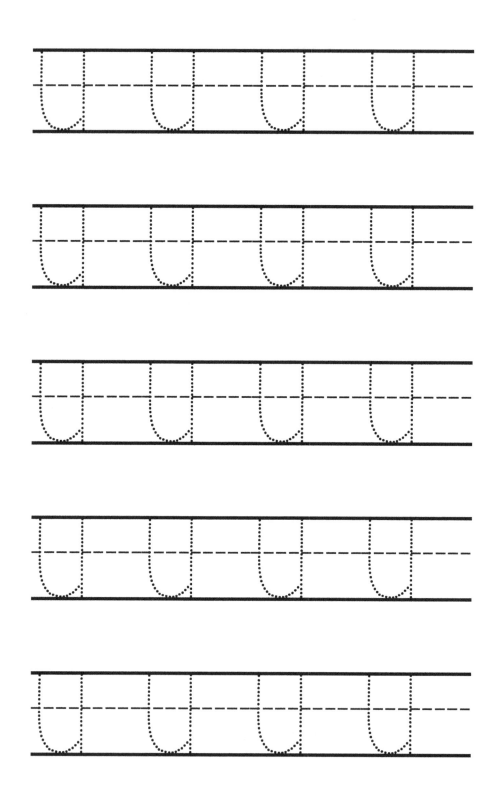

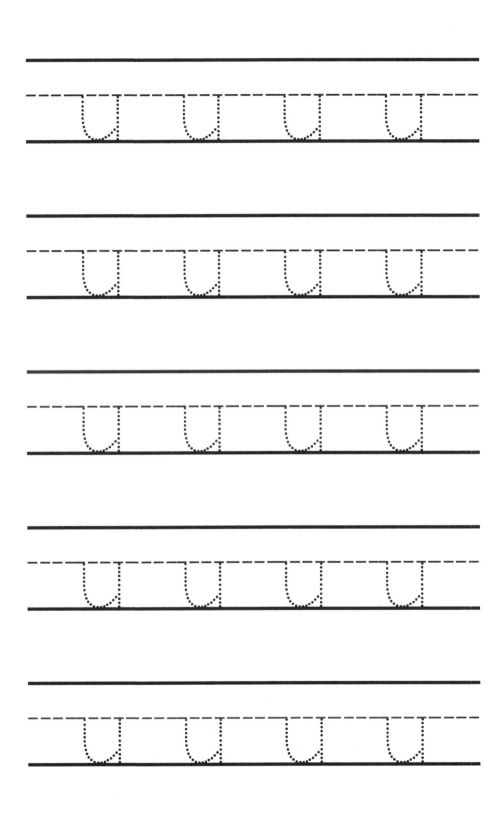

The Letter V

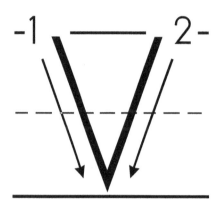

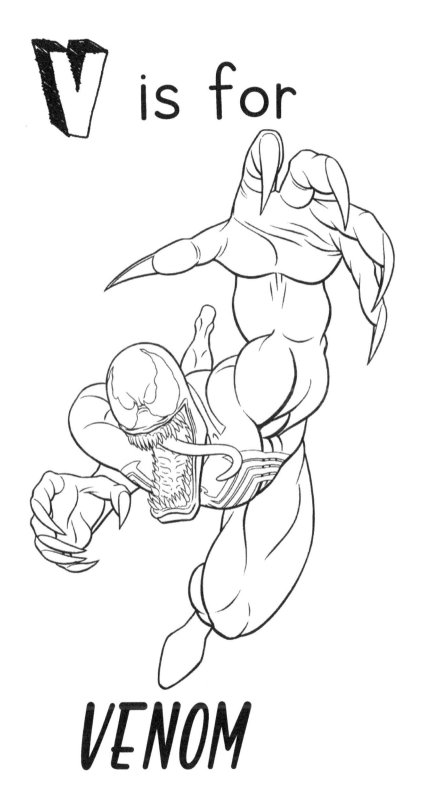

V is for VENOM

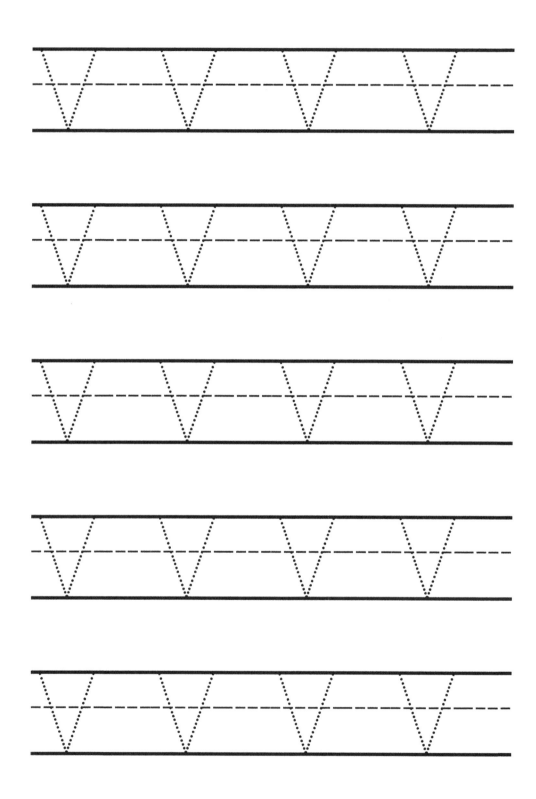

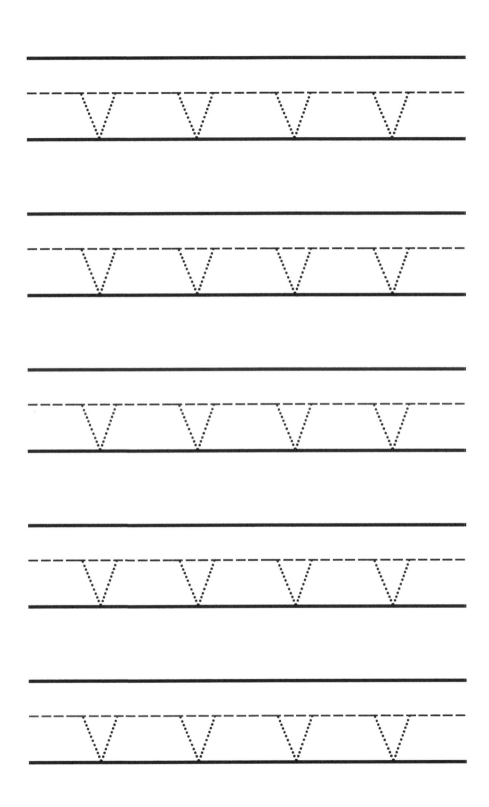

The Letter W

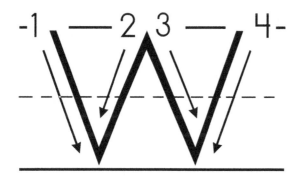 

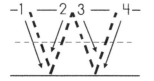 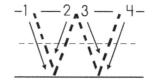 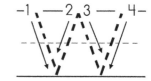

W is for

WOLVERINE

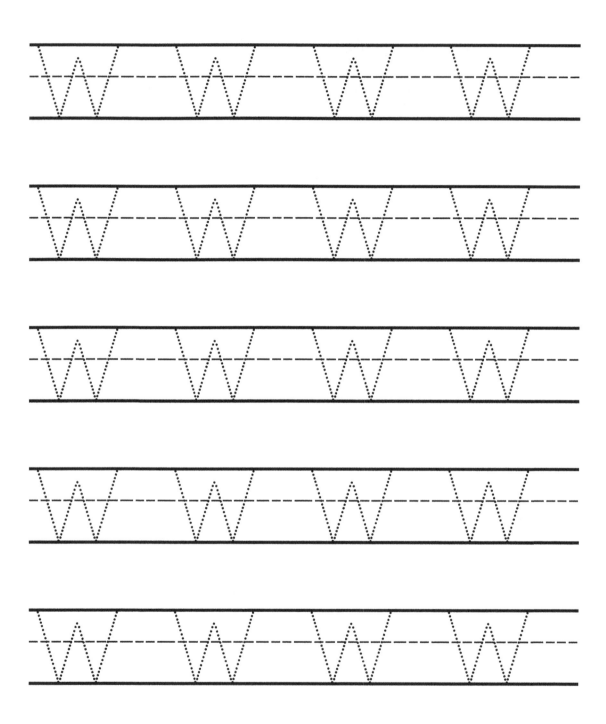

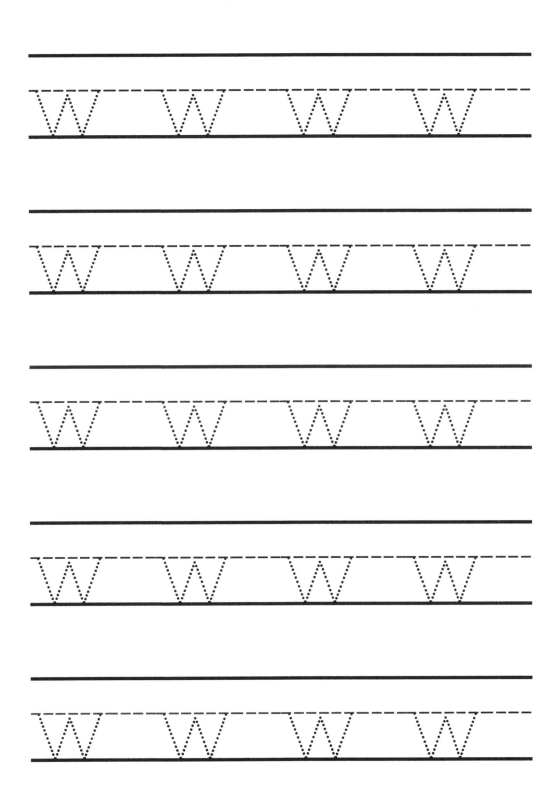

The Letter X

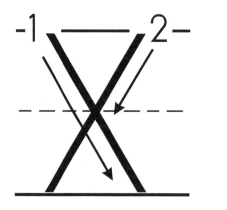
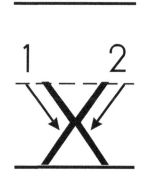

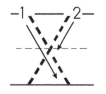

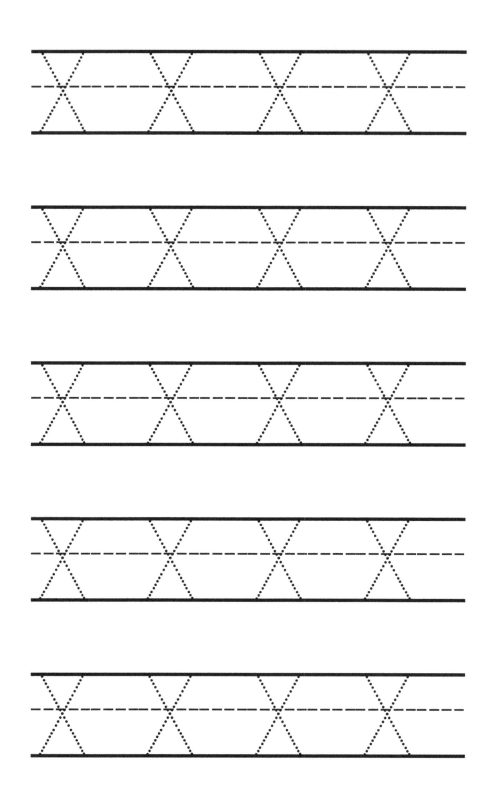

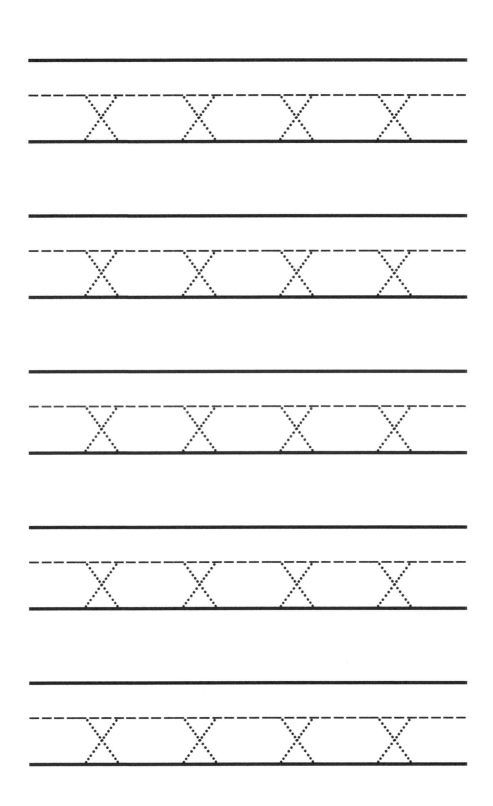

The Letter Y

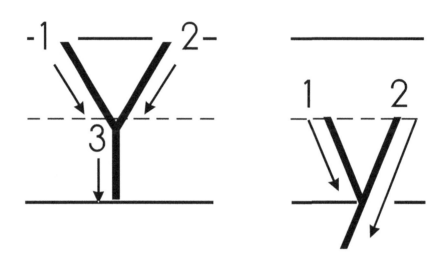

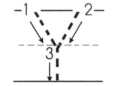 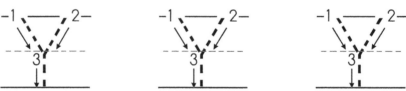 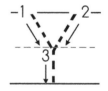

Y is for

YODA

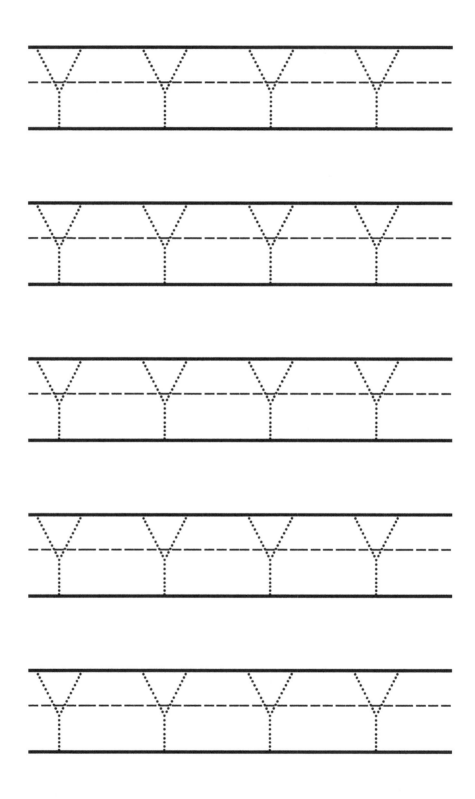

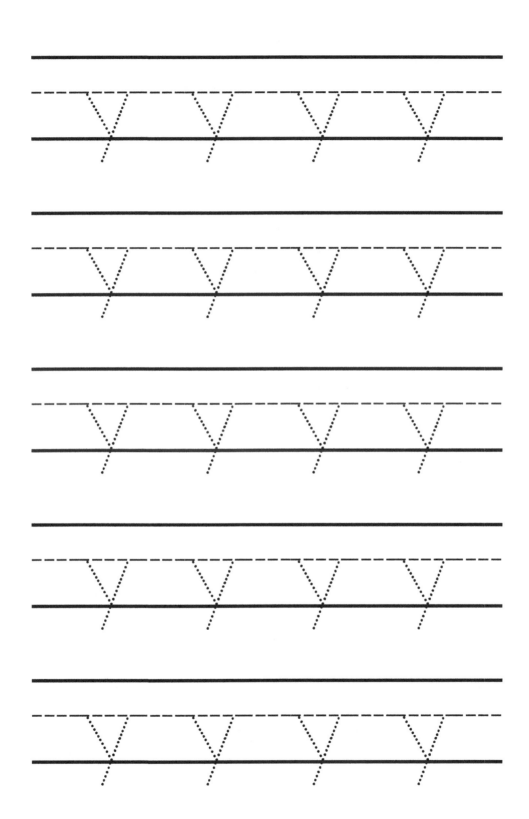

The Letter Z

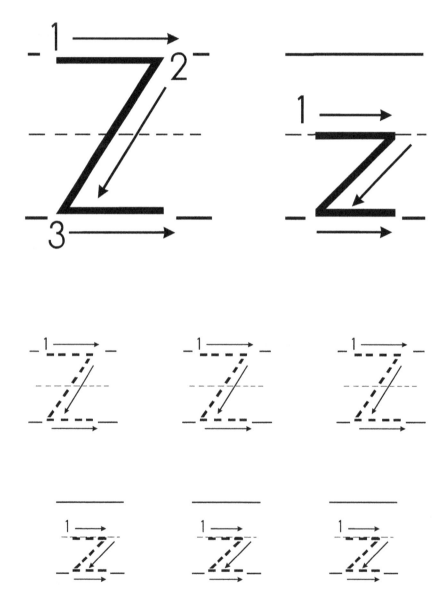

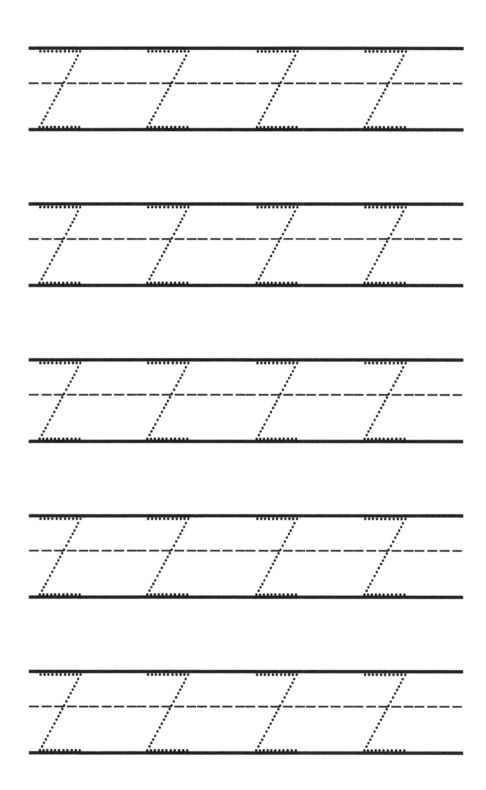

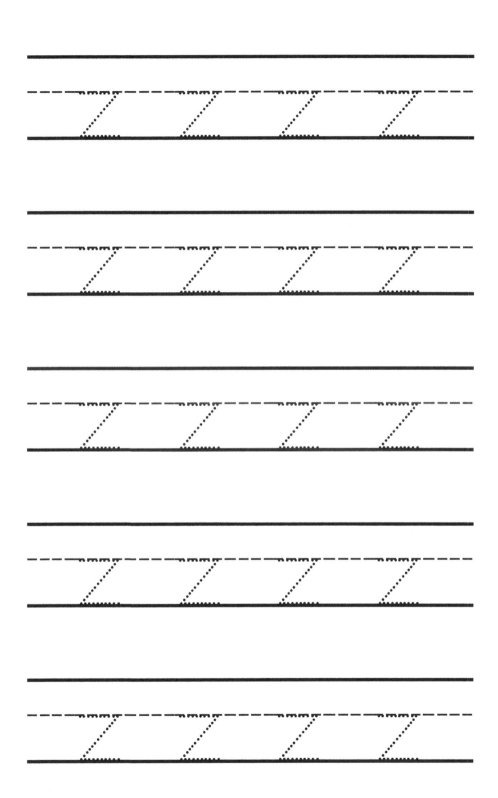

Made in the USA
Las Vegas, NV
14 July 2021